Windsor Castle

A Royal Residence for 900 Years

Windsor Castle has belonged continuously to the sovereigns of England since the days of the Norman Conquest over 900 years ago and its present occupant, Her Majesty Queen Elizabeth II, is a direct descendant of its founder. It was not as a stone-walled castle but as a typical Norman stronghold of earth and timber that it first existed, one of many constructed by the forces of William the Conqueror to control the country after his invasion of 1066.

The castle formed one of a ring of garrisons built to command the area around London, each a day's march from its neighbours and from the centre. The site at Windsor was of strategic importance, because it dominated the Thames, then the main freight route into the interior. The fortifications erected upon it were made unusually long and narrow so as to take advantage of a lengthy escarpment.

The site was also on the edge of a vast tract of royal forest in which the Saxon kings had hunted for centuries, with a small hunting lodge four miles downstream, in an ancient settlement called Windlesora. The Norman invaders enjoyed the hunt no less and named the new fortress after it.

Over the years Windsor became increasingly important as a royal residence. Henry I is recorded as having held his court here in 1110.

LEFT: *King Edward lll (1327–77), founder of the Most Noble Order of the Garter.*

RIGHT: *A banquet of the Knights of the Garter in the original St George's Hall, built by King Edward lll in 1362–5.*

BELOW: *A scene showing a Royal feast being prepared in Windsor Castle's great medieval kitchen.*

BELOW LEFT: *A view of Windsor Castle from the east, showing the original steep escarpment of the fortress and the terrace built by King Charles ll in the 1670s.*

It was more than 50 years later, during the reign of his grandson Henry II, before the occupants were able to enjoy the luxury of stone buildings. Henry II built his domestic apartments in the Lower Ward and those for ceremonial purposes in the Upper Ward. These were destroyed by fire a little over a century later, and since then the Royal apartments have been confined to the Upper Ward of the castle.

Later in Henry's reign a rebellion started by his two sons, Richard and John, forced the king to strengthen the castle's defences. The lower half of the Round Tower probably dates from this time, as well as much of the Upper Ward, with its rectangular towers, and the walls around the Middle and Lower Wards.

The castle suffered two sieges during this period. The most serious of these was the barons' rebellion against John in 1216 after he persuaded the Pope to annul the Magna Carta, the charter which ever since has affirmed the individual's right to justice and liberty. The castle came under heavy attack for three months and its walls were badly damaged.

Early in Henry III's reign the damage to the castle was repaired, the perimeter wall completed and the circular towers added. On the domestic side no fewer than four major reconstructions followed. The first, by Henry III in the 1240s, took 20 years and was the last word in luxury for the age, but apart from a chapel, these buildings did not survive.

In 1348 King Edward III, inspired by the legends of King Arthur and the Knights of the Round Table, founded the Most Noble Order of the Garter, Britain's highest order of chivalry. The new order, consisting of 26 Knights Companion, swore personal allegiance to the king and adopted St George as their patron saint. The knights worshipped in Henry III's existing chapel and spectacular new apartments were built for their use, including the original St George's Hall, where the knights met on St George's Day for their ceremonial banquet. The king also built extensive quarters for the clergy.

It was Edward's royal successor, Edward IV, who began the construction of the present chapel of St George in 1475 as a setting worthy of the order, but it was not until 50 years later, in the reign of Henry VIII, that this masterpiece of late Perpendicular Gothic architecture was completed. St George's Chapel replaced its predecessor as the Chapel of the Order of the Garter and still provides a magnificent setting for the Garter service today.

More than a century later, when the Civil War broke out in 1642, King Charles I fled to York, making no attempt to defend his stronghold. The castle fell into the hands of Oliver Cromwell's Parliamentary forces. They stole plate and treasures from St George's Chapel, evicted the dean and canons from their houses and stabled their horses in the nave. The castle became a gaol for Royalist prisoners.

Charles did not see his castle again until he was brought back to it as a prisoner. Leaders of the Parliamentary army, including Cromwell, had met at Windsor and taken the fateful decision 'that the king should be prosecuted for his life as a criminal person'. The doomed king spent his last Christmas in captivity here, in 1648, shortly before his trial and execution. Charles's body was brought back to the castle and buried in St George's Chapel. The burial took place in silence as the Parliamentary authorities would not allow the use of the funeral service prescribed in the Book of Common Prayer, and the location of the king's tomb remained unknown for over a century and a half.

After the Restoration, King Charles II commissioned the architect Hugh May to replace the royal apartments with a new palace in the fashionable baroque style. The basic structure of this building survives in the present State Apartments but a century and a half later a monarch came to the throne whose visions of grandeur eclipsed those of any of his predecessors.

This was George IV, whose architect Sir Jeffry Wyatville carried out the castle's last and greatest reconstruction. Charles II's elegant apartments were retained with much of their original decoration but George IV built new private apartments for himself on the other two sides of the Upper Ward. The larger rooms in the castle were remodelled for ceremonial use. All the new work was dominated by the gothic style, the external additions including an extra storey on the Round Tower, several completely new towers, and a profusion of elaborate battlements, turrets and towers, giving the castle its dramatic air of romantic medievalism.

So successful was the design of this great reconstruction and so sound the workmanship that little alteration has been needed since. The basic structure of the palace left to his successors by George IV is much the same as that used by Queen Elizabeth II today.

RIGHT: *A bird's-eye view of Windsor Castle showing King Edward III's Royal apartments and the original St George's Hall (numbered 17 on the roof) grouped around the Quadrangle. St George's Chapel can be seen on the left in Lower Ward. The moat and drawbridge are also visible.*

BELOW RIGHT: *North-west view of Windsor Castle from the bank of the river Thames, 19th century.*

BELOW: *The funeral procession of King Charles I, 8 February 1649, at the steps of St George's Chapel. The king's funeral took place without a service on the orders of Oliver Cromwell.*

Profpect of the Castle from the S.E.

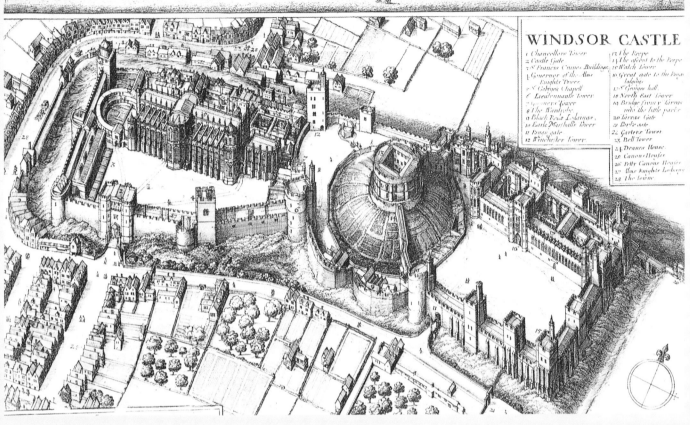

WINDSOR CASTLE

1 Chancellors Tower
2 Castle Gate
3 S.t Francis Crane's Buildings
4 Gouernor of the Alms
Knights Tower
5 S.t Georges Chapell
6 Lieutenants Tower
7 Spencers Tower
8 The Wardrobe
9 Black Rods Lodgings
10 Earle Marshalls Tower
11 Ennes gate
12 Winchester Tower
13 The Keepe
14 The afcent to the Keepe
15 Watch Tower
16 Great gate to the Kings
lodging
17 S.t Georges hall
18 North East Tower
19 Bridge from y.e Terras
into the little parke
20 Terras Gate
21 Parke gate
22 Garters Tower
23 Bell Tower
24 Deanes House
25 Canon House
26 Petty Canons Houses
27 Poor Knights Lodgings
28 The Towne

5

Tour of the Castle Precincts

The Middle Ward

Crowning the Middle Ward is the Round Tower, built as the main stronghold of the castle by King Henry II in the 12th century, on a mound raised by William the Conqueror at the time of the castle's foundation in the 1070s when a strategic site was chosen overlooking the river Thames.

The Round Tower formed the central feature of the original fortress with its surrounding dry moat, walls and towers. The tower is not strictly circular in form: its longest diameter measures 103 feet (31.3m) and its shortest 94 feet (28.6m). The lower half, as far as the coping above the large windows, is thought to have been built about 1170, 100 years after the raising of the artificial mound on which it stands. Before this the summit had been fortified with a wooden structure. The upper half was added for King

ABOVE: *The massive Round Tower in Middle Ward is Windsor Castle's famous landmark.*

LEFT: *The twin towers of the Norman Gate with the Moat Garden in the foreground.*

George IV in 1828–32. The top of the tower stands 215 feet (65.5m) above the river Thames and 280 feet (85.3m) above sea level. The Union Jack is flown from the top of the Round Tower, and is replaced by the much larger Royal Standard when The Queen visits the castle.

The ditch below the Round Tower is occupied by a delightful garden belonging to the Governor of the castle, whose residence stands beside it. The Moat Garden is where King James I saw and fell in love with Lady Joan Beaufort. The king, a prisoner in the castle for 11 years

(1413–24), saw the lady walking in the garden, fell in love with her, and later married her. The king wrote a poem in which he tells of his love and describes the 'gardyn faire'.

Beside the Round Tower stand the twin towers of the Norman Gate, built by King Edward III in the 14th century to replace an earlier gateway defending access to the Upper Ward, where the domestic quarters of the sovereign were, and still are, situated. The portcullis, which was let down between grooves from the room above, is still in place above the outer arch.

The Upper Ward

The Norman Gate leads into a small courtyard in the Upper Ward known as Engine Court. On the left is a gallery constructed by Queen Elizabeth I in the 16th century, followed by a building erected a century earlier by her grandfather King Henry VII as quarters for his queen and family. All these buildings now house the Royal Library.

Engine Court looks on to the vast open courtyard known as the Quadrangle. The Changing of the Guard takes place on this magnificent expanse of lawn during the official residence of The Queen. The Quadrangle also forms an impressive setting for colourful Royal pageantry on the occasion of a State Visit, when there is a vast procession consisting of carriages accompanied by the Household Cavalry and a Guard of Honour with a regimental band.

On the left can be seen the State Apartments and the State Entrance and on the right are the Private Apartments of The Queen. The Sover-

LEFT: *Ceremonial cannons flank the South Terrace.*

RIGHT: *The East Front of Windsor Castle and the beautiful formal garden created in the Italian style for King George IV.*

BELOW: *The vast Quadrangle is the perfect setting for the Changing of the Guard as well as horse-mounted processions during State Visits.*

eign's Entrance is situated in the opposite corner to Engine Court.

The Quadrangle as it appears today is largely the work of King George IV's architect Sir Jeffry Wyatville, who completed a large reconstruction of the Upper Ward in the 1820s. The intention was to return to the medieval architectural style of Edward III but with the additional comforts of a great 19th-century country house. Wyatville added the numerous windows and the romantic gothic towers and battlements.

The Round Tower was doubled in height at this time and in its turn adorned with battlements. The Long Walk to the south of the castle, begun by King Charles II, was completed and extended into the Quadrangle through an imposing new gateway, King George IV Gate. In addition, the Grand Corridor was built to link all the rooms on the south and east fronts (the Royal Apartments). The handsome equestrian statue of Charles II, erected in the centre of the Quadrangle in 1680, was moved to its present position beneath the Round Tower.

The North Terrace can be reached either by walking down the steps beneath the Royal Library, or from Middle Ward through an opening in the outer wall of the castle. The North Terrace, built by King Charles II in the 17th century, commands a panoramic view of the Thames Valley, with Eton College and the Chiltern Hills beyond.

Originally there was no terrace on the north front of the castle, which rose directly above a sheer escarpment – a terrace would have weakened its defences. In 1533 King Henry VIII built a terrace made of wood, which was replaced by a stone structure for Queen Elizabeth I in 1574–78 and altered in the 1670s by Charles II to extend around the outside of the east and south sides of the Quadrangle.

When members of the Royal Family are not in residence the far end of the North Terrace leads to a point from which the East Front of the castle and the formal garden below it can be seen. The public has access to this view-point again now that work to the fire-damaged parts of the castle has been completed. The superb Italian-style garden, complete with terraces, fountain and orangery, was created for King George IV on an exposed and east-facing hilltop site. This was made possible by enclosing it within a raised stone wall whose top was level with, and provided an extension of, the terraces. This gives it the appearance of a sunken garden, while protecting it from the keen winds.

The Lower Ward

To reach the Lower Ward the visitor must return along the North Terrace to Middle Ward and the foot of the Round Tower. On the right, beyond the Deanery, stands the Albert Memorial Chapel. St George's Chapel is situated further down the hill on the right and is entered by the south porch. A passageway between the two chapels leads to the Dean's Cloister and beyond it to the Canons' Cloister, both dating from the 14th century.

On the other side of the Lower Ward from the Albert Memorial Chapel and St George's Chapel stand the residences of the Military Knights, a foundation instituted by King Edward III in connection with the Order of the Garter and pro-viding lodgings for retired army officers who have served with distinction. Dressed in a scarlet uniform conferred on them by King William IV in the 19th century, they attend Morning Service in St George's Chapel on Sundays, and play an important part in the ceremonial of the chapel on royal occasions.

The square tower in the centre of the range, Mary Tudor Tower, which was built as a belfry in the 14th century and bears the arms of Mary Tudor and her husband King Philip of Spain, is the residence of their Governor. The next house downhill used to contain their dining hall, and bears a representation of the Garter over its front door. The houses below it were built in the reign of Mary Tudor (1553–8). The upper range was

RIGHT: *Henry VIII Gate.*

BELOW: *Henry VIII's arms, together with a Tudor rose, and a pomegranate, badge of his first queen, Catherine of Aragon, can be seen over the arch of Henry VIII Gate.*

LEFT: *The 15th-century timber-framed houses in the Horseshoe Cloister were restored in the 19th century by Sir George Gilbert Scott.*

RIGHT: *Castle Hill, where the Changing of the Guard can sometimes be seen.*

BELOW: *The Garter Badge is displayed on the house of the Superintendent of Windsor Castle, on the south side of Lower Ward.*

originally constructed 200 years earlier by King Edward III for members of the clergy.

In the far right-hand corner of Lower Ward is a small gateway leading to the Horseshoe Cloister, a row of timber-framed houses originally built by King Edward IV in approximately 1480 for the priest-vicars of St George's Chapel and now housing the men singers of the chapel choir and the vergers. The cloister owes its present appearance to a restoration by Sir George Gilbert Scott in the 19th century. Opposite lies the Great West Door of St George's Chapel.

Beyond the far corner of the cloister lies the Curfew Tower. Built in 1227 as part of the last section of the outer wall to be completed, the tower contains a fine example of a medieval dungeon in the basement as well as one end of a secret underground passage or 'sally port', extending out beneath the castle wall, of which the far end is blocked.

The upper storey contains the eight bells of St George's Chapel. These are chimed every three hours through a mechanism operated by a clock dating from the 17th century. The conical roof was added in 1863.

Another gateway at the far side of the cloister leads to an area which contains residences of clergy and others connected with St George's Chapel. All these buildings are closed to the public but from the terrace there is a fine view of the river Thames and of Eton beyond it.

On the right, in front of the Guard Room, lies the Parade Ground, where the Changing of the Guard takes place in winter. The impressive gateway to Windsor Castle, where the visitor's tour ends, is known as King Henry VIII Gate, built in 1511 when the castle was already more than 400 years old. The vault of the arch is pierced by holes through which boiling oil could be poured on attackers during a siege. A drawbridge used to lead over a ditch encircling the castle.

PARKING
FOR
PERMIT
HOLDERS
ONLY

11

The Albert Memorial Chapel

The Albert Memorial Chapel stands on the site of the earlier chapel built by King Henry III in 1240 and used by Edward III when he founded the Order of the Garter in the middle of the following century. The exterior was originally constructed by Henry VII in the late 15th century as a Lady Chapel for St George's Chapel. He intended it as a shrine for the remains of the saintly King Henry VI and for his own tomb but it was not used for either of these purposes and the chapel fell into disuse for many years.

The richly decorated interior of the chapel was created for Queen Victoria in 1863–73 as a memorial to her husband, Albert, the Prince Consort, who died in 1861 at the age of only 42. The chapel is the work of Sir George Gilbert Scott and houses a marble effigy of Prince Albert, whose tomb is in the Royal Mausoleum at Frogmore. Queen Victoria went into mourning for her beloved young husband for 40 years and according to her wishes the Queen's remains joined Albert's on her death in 1901. The illustrated panels around the walls of the chapel depict scenes from the Bible.

RIGHT: *Interior of the Albert Memorial Chapel, exquisitely decorated in the high-Victorian style. The Chapel contains the marble effigy of Queen Victoria's Consort Prince Albert.*

LEFT: *The Albert Memorial Chapel commemorates Albert, the Prince Consort (above), who died in 1861 of typhoid. The young Queen Victoria (below) mourned her dear husband for 40 years.*

BELOW: *The Albert Memorial Chapel in Lower Ward.*

St George's Chapel

St George's Chapel, one of the finest examples of the Perpendicular style of late gothic architecture, was founded in 1475 by King Edward IV as the chapel of the Order of the Garter and completed 50 years later by King Henry VIII. The chapel is in regular use on great ceremonial occasions and the most important of these is the service of the Order of the Garter. This historic pageant takes place in early June when The Queen and the 26 Knights Companion, attired in the robes of the Order, walk in procession from the castle through the Norman Gate and the Middle and Lower Wards, to enter the Great West Door of the Chapel for the annual service.

The Order, which was founded in 1348 by King Edward III, is Britain's highest order of chivalry and is said to have its origin in a charming story. Tradition has it that at a ball held to celebrate the capture of Calais in 1387 a lady's garter fell to the ground. The king picked it up and, seeing his courtiers smile, said, 'Honi soit qui mal y pense' – 'Shame on him who thinks evil of it'. These words became the motto of the Order.

The procession is led by the heralds, wearing richly embroidered scarlet coatees, black breeches and stockings and buckled court shoes. A tabard embroidered with the royal arms is also worn and the heralds carry ceremonial swords. The knights and heralds are joined in procession by the Military Knights of Windsor, who wear scarlet tunics with gold epaulettes and plumed cocked hats. The Sovereign is attended by The Queen's Bodyguard in gold and scarlet uniforms with white collar ruffs and Tudor bonnets dating from 1552. They carry ceremonial pikestaffs. The route is lined by soldiers of the Household Cavalry and the Guards Division.

The Knights include the Duke of Edinburgh, the Prince of Wales, the Princess Royal and Prince William. Their robes consist of a blue velvet mantle (cloak) with white ribbons, a plumed velvet cap, a scarlet sash embroidered with the badge of the Order, an enamelled collar of gold knots, Tudor roses and Garters with a pendant of St George and the Dragon (patron saint of England and of the Order) and the badge itself – the Garter Star on a blue riband. The blue garter which gave the Order its name is worn buckled below the left knee. This is embroidered with the motto of the Order.

RIGHT: *The banners of the Knights of the Garter hang beneath the magnificent fan-vaulted ceiling in the Choir of St George's Chapel, burial place of ten sovereigns.*

ABOVE: *The Queen and the Duke of Edinburgh are joined by Queen Elizabeth the Queen Mother and the Prince of Wales at the Great West Door of St George's Chapel after the service of the Order of the Garter.*

LEFT: *The Queen wearing the robes of the Order and the Garter Star with St George's Cross.*

The State Apartments

The Grand Staircase

The visitor enters the newly-refurbished State Apartments via the imposing Grand Staircase. Originally a medieval herb garden, the site remained an open courtyard until the 1820s, when it was enclosed by a staircase designed by Sir Jeffry Wyatville. This was replaced by the present staircase, designed by the architect Anthony Salvin for Queen Victoria, in 1866. The stairwell is dominated by a huge marble statue by Sir Francis Chantrey of King George IV, the monarch largely responsible for the present appearance of the castle. On either side of the landing at the top of the staircase stand two small suits of armour, made for the sons of King James I.

The Grand Vestibule

The next room which the visitor enters is the Grand Vestibule. This room owes its strange shape to the fact that it was designed as the landing for the earlier staircase. The gothic vaulting was designed by James Wyatt (uncle of Sir Jeffry Wyatville) and the lantern and decorated ceiling can still be seen. The room is now used for the display of militaria. In the case to the left of the exit to the Grand Staircase are relics of Tipoo Sultan, King of Mysore, including a gold tiger's head which formed part of his throne. The case on the opposite wall contains Napoleonic relics, including a sword used by Napoleon Bonaparte when First Consul and the bullet which killed Nelson at the Battle of Trafalgar in 1805.

BELOW: *The Grand Staircase.*

The Waterloo Chamber

The Waterloo Chamber is the outcome of a grand scheme by King George IV to commemorate the allied victory over Napoleon at Waterloo. The king's architect Sir Jeffry Wyatville created the impressive banqueting hall with its remarkable clerestory to accommodate the series of paintings, by Sir Thomas Lawrence, of all the monarchs, statesmen and soldiers who had played a part in Napoleon's defeat. The 38 paintings are dominated by the magnificent portrait of the victor of Waterloo, Arthur, Duke of Wellington, shown wearing the Order of the Garter and holding the Sword of State. Behind 16 of them are now revealed pantomime character cartoons. These were painted on wallpaper in 1944 by a 15-year-old student, Claude Whatham, to accompany a pantomime devised and acted by The Queen (when Princess Elizabeth), Princess Margaret and others in the castle community. Many of the woodcarvings are by Grinling Gibbons. The huge carpet, reputed to be the largest seamless carpet in Europe, was made for Queen Victoria at Agra in India.

The magnificent table seats up to 60 guests and is used for banquets held in the presence of The Queen on the occasion of State Visits and the annual gathering of the Order of the Garter.

The Garter Throne Room

The Garter Throne Room was constructed for King George IV by Wyatville in one of the oldest parts of the castle, dating from the 12th century. During the reign of King Charles II the far end of the room, where the throne is situated, was a separate chamber where the king gave audience. Today the Knights of the Garter assemble here in June, in the presence of The Queen, to conduct their business, which includes the investiture of new knights, before the procession through the castle precincts to St George's Chapel for the annual service. Set into the walls are portraits of sovereigns in their Garter robes, from King George I to Queen Victoria. Over the fireplace hangs the state portrait of Queen Elizabeth II by James Gunn. The fine woodcarvings are by Grinling Gibbons.

The King's Drawing Room

In the next room, the King's Drawing Room, the pictures are all by Rubens and his school. Over the fireplace is *The Holy Family,* flanked by a landscape depicting summer and a scene of peasants in a barn depicting winter. The equestrian portrait to the left of the entrance, after Rubens, is Philip II of Spain, who married Mary I of England in 1554. The ceiling is decorated with the Order of the Garter Star and garter badges. It was in this room that the body of King George IV lay in state after his death in 1830.

The King's State Bedchamber

The King's State Bedchamber became the principal bedroom of the royal apartments in the reign of King George IV. The initials of King Charles II appear in the corners of the ceiling. The French 18th-century bed was placed here by Queen Victoria for the State Visit of Napoleon III and the Empress Eugenie in 1855. The Empire-style hangings are in the Napoleonic colours of purple and green and the foot of the bed bears their monograms. Around the walls hang a superb series of pictures of Venice by Canaletto, part of a collection of 50 paintings and 140 drawings by the artist purchased by King George III in 1762 from Joseph Smith, British Consul in Venice.

The King's Dressing Room

The King's Dressing Room was originally much larger and served as a small private bedroom for King Charles II. Sir Jeffry Wyatville converted it into a dressing room for royal guests during the reconstruction carried out for King George IV. The pictures in this room are some of the finest in the Royal Collection. They include portraits by Rubens, Rembrandt, Holbein, Durer and Van Dyck. The most famous of these is Van Dyck's triple portrait of King Charles I, which hangs over the fireplace. This was commissioned and sent to Rome to enable the sculptor Bernini to carve a bust of the king.

The King's Closet

The King's Closet served King Charles II as a private sitting room but Wyatville converted it into a private bedroom in the suite for royal guests. The fine 18th-century pictures include Canaletto's painting of Venice, from King George III's 1762 purchase. The portraits hanging in this room are by Sir Joshua Reynolds, Allan Ramsay and William Hogarth. Hogarth's work is of the famous 18th-century actor David Garrick.

The Queen's Drawing Room

The Queen's Drawing Room was first constructed by King Charles II for Queen Catherine of Braganza as her 'withdrawing room' or private sitting room. After conversion it formed a drawing room for visitors. The room is hung with fine portraits of the Tudor and Stuart monarchs. King Henry VIII, King Edward VI, Queen Mary I, Queen Elizabeth I and Sir Henry Guildford are by or after Hans Holbein. The state portrait of King James I by Paul van Somer hangs on the left of the exit and on the right is his son King Charles I by Daniel Mytens. The painting over the fireplace depicts King James's elder son, Henry, Prince of Wales (died 1612) in a hunting scene.

The King's Dining Room

The King's Dining Room is one of three existing apartments designed in the baroque style by Hugh May for King Charles II in 1675–83. The room has a magnificent ceiling painted by the Italian artist Antonio Verrio and remarkable decorative carvings by the famous woodcarver Grinling Gibbons. Verrio's painting, completed in 1678, is of a banquet of the gods, a theme echoed in the carvings, which show flowers, fruit, fish and game. A portrait by Jacob Huysmans of King Charles II's queen, Catherine of Braganza, hangs above the fireplace. On the left near the doorway stands a fine terracotta bust of King Charles himself.

ABOVE: *The King's Drawing Room.*

RIGHT: *The King's State Bedchamber.*

18

The Queen's Ballroom

The Queen's Ballroom was created for Queen Catherine of Braganza in the 1670s but owes its present appearance to King George IV. The room was known for over a hundred years as the Van Dyck Room because of its pictures and more recently these magnificent paintings have returned here. Among them is Van Dyck's popular portrait of the five eldest children of King Charles I, and the artist's handsome state portrait of King Charles I.

The Queen's Audience Chamber

The Queen's Audience Chamber is the second of the three rooms (*see the King's Dining Room*) in King Charles II's baroque palace which retains its 17th-century appearance. Queen Catherine of Braganza would have had a throne in this room and it is here that she would have given audience. On the ceiling Queen Catherine is depicted by Antonio Verrio in a chariot drawn by swans to the Temple of Virtue. The magnificent tapestries in this and the following room were woven at the Gobelins factory in France in the 1780s. They depict the story of Esther, the Jewish queen of Ahasuerus, King of the Persians, who saved her compatriots from the massacre ordered by her husband. The painting above the entrance door is of William II, Prince of Orange, father of King William III. The portrait above the exit is of Mary Queen of Scots. The woodcarvings which surround the pictures are by Grinling Gibbons.

The Queen's Presence Chamber

The Queen's Presence Chamber is the third room which survives as designed for King Charles II in the 17th century. The superb ceiling portrays Queen Catherine of Braganza surrounded by virtues, while below her the sword of Justice banishes vices such as Sedition and Envy. Most of the other rooms in the State Apartments were similarly decorated by Antonio Verrio but only those in this room, the Queen's Audience Chamber and the King's Dining Room survive; the others were lost during later restorations. The marble fireplace, brought here from Buckingham Palace by King William IV, was designed by Robert Adam in 1789. The portrait above it by Pierre Mignard depicts Charlotte, Duchess of Orleans, a first cousin of King George I, with her children. The woodcarvings are by Grinling Gibbons. On the left of the entrance is a bust of the composer George Frederick Handel, whose music was often played at concerts given in this room by King George III.

The Queen's Guard Chamber

The Queen's Guard Chamber housed the guard past which visitors seeking audience with Queen Catherine had to pass. It was reconstructed by King George IV to display militaria. In the centre stands the figure of the King's Champion, who used to ride fully armed into the coronation banquet and challenge all present to deny the title of the new sovereign. On either side stand fine busts of John, Duke of Marlborough and Arthur, Duke of Wellington, each surmounted by a small standard, one bearing the arms of the kings of France, and the other the tricolor. These are rendered annually by the present dukes as token rent for their estates, Blenheim Palace and Stratfield Saye, in commemoration of their ancestors' victories over the French.

LEFT: *The Queen's Ballroom.*

ABOVE: *The Queen's Guard Chamber.*

After The Fire

Even while firemen were dousing down the burning embers the morning after the fire, the restoration process was already beginning, under the direction of The Royal Household Property Section, reporting to The Queen and The Duke of Edinburgh. Both Prince Philip and The Prince of Wales took a keen interest in the work being done: each chaired a separate committee, advising how the principal rooms should be restored and recommending the architect for the new designs.

It was decided to return the State Apartments to their original glory, to redesign the Private Chapel area, the ceiling and East Screen area of St George's Hall, and to rationalize the tangle of rooms in the service areas.

The work was originally scheduled to be completed in spring 1998, with a ceiling budget of £40 million. Most of this was met from opening Buckingham Palace for two months in the summer, while the rest came from Royal funds. The first task was to make safe the charred and

ABOVE: *Part of the stained glass window, based on a design by The Duke of Edinburgh, in the Private Chapel. A worker rescues a portrait of Wyatville.*

22

LEFT: *The Lantern Lobby, with the plaque marking where the fire started.*

RIGHT: *St George's Hall. The new arched ceiling is made from green oak, with 980 shields of the Garter Knights between the trusses.*

LEFT: *The Grand Reception Room restored to its original opulent splendour. The veneer on the malachite urn flaked off in the fire and was meticulously pieced back together.*

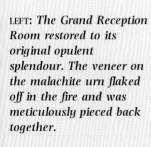

ABOVE: *A skilled plasterer restores the gilded plaster cove in the Grand Reception Room.*

smoking remains before archaeologists could painstakingly sift through the debris, stored in over 7,000 dustbins, for fragments that could either be used again or reproduced. Over three-quarters of the pieces from the cut glass chandelier in the Crimson Drawing Room were salvaged in this way. The inside of the building, doused with water for 15 hours, had to be dried out before any work could begin and, to speed up the process, historic wall linings were carefully removed. This revealed earlier parts of the Castle's history, including the remains of a mural in St George's Hall which had been painted by Antonio Verrio for Charles II.

The new St George's Hall ceiling is in a modern Gothic style with arched trusses replacing Sir Jeffry Wyatville's flat ceiling from the 19th century. The octagonal Lantern Lobby is also Gothic in design, with clusters of oak shafts fanning out in lily-head vaults towards the glazed lantern in the ceiling. A new Private Chapel was built in the area formerly known as the Holbein Room with an altar table designed by David Linley, The Queen's nephew.

The skills of over 4,000 workers were employed in the restoration and the work was finished ahead of schedule and within budget. On 20 November 1997, exactly five years since the fire and on the Golden Wedding Anniversary of The Queen and The Duke of Edinburgh, a celebratory ball was held in rooms that can once again be admired in all their splendour.

Queen Mary's Dolls' House

Queen Mary's Dolls' House must be the most magnificent dolls' house in the world, an English country mansion in miniature. The house, designed by the famous architect Sir Edwin Lutyens as a gift for Queen Mary, was intended to be a work of the finest English craftsmanship, a model of an early 20th-century royal residence perfect in every detail.

Built on a scale of 1 to 12 (or one-twelfth normal size), the house is a miracle of scale and accuracy. The fixtures and fittings are extremely up-to-date for a house of its age. It has electric lighting, hot and cold running water, and fully-operating lifts and door locks. It boasts an electric vacuum cleaner, an electric iron and a Singer sewing-machine. The exterior of the house, decorated to resemble Portland stone, has sliding sash windows.

The finest materials were used in the construction of the house and its contents. It has marble stairs, floors and bathrooms, 'Queen Anne' and 'Chippendale' furniture, jade ornaments, silk curtains, a silver table service and even the 'Crown Jewels' securely stowed in a Strong Room. The traditional Wine Cellar is stocked with famous vintages of champagne, claret and brandy.

The Library contains leather-bound volumes by many famous authors and poets, among them Rudyard Kipling, Arthur Conan Doyle and A. E. Housman, and a large collection of prints, water-colours and drawings by well-known artists.

The garage has six vintage motor-cars, including a Rolls Royce Silver Ghost, and all the tools and equipment necessary for their maintenance. There are even two miniature perambulators and a bicycle. The formal garden was designed by the great English gardener Gertrude Jekyll.

The house was finally completed in 1924 after three years' painstaking work, with 1,500 craftsmen, artists and authors contributing to Lutyens' grand design. It went on display at the British Empire Exhibition in that year, and the following year was brought to Windsor Castle.

BELOW: *A diminutive wine bottle made in perfect proportion. All the objects in the Dolls' House are made on a scale of 1 to 12 (or one-twelfth normal size).*

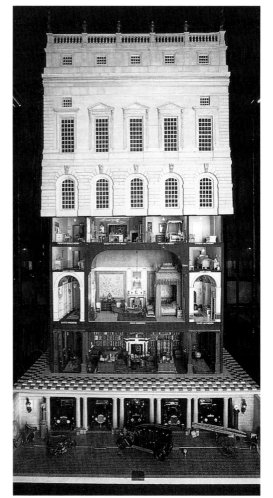

FAR LEFT: *The west front of the Dolls' House showing the King's Bedroom and the Library with the garage below.*

ABOVE: *In the Dining Room the table is laid with silver and crystal.*

LEFT: *The exquisite workmanship in these tiny golf clubs and bag, which is 2½ inches long, is typical of every detail in the Dolls' House.*

The Gallery

The Gallery provides a rare and superb opportunity to view exquisite watercolours, drawings, books and a variety of precious objects from The Queen's collection.

The exhibits, from the Royal Library, form part of the Royal Collection, one of the finest art collections in the world. Works on display may include items from the outstanding collection of Old Master Drawings, encompassing Leonardo, Raphael, Michelangelo and Canaletto, portraits of leading figures of the 20th century, and delightful views of Windsor town, castle and Great Park in earlier days by the 18th-century watercolourists Thomas and Paul Sandby.

The Gallery was sympathetically refurbished in 1992 by Alec Cobbe with new exhibition furniture, hangings and lighting designed to harmonize with the original neo-gothic architecture. The aisled, rib-vaulted lobby was designed by Sir Jeffry Wyatville for King George IV as the entrance to the Grand Staircase leading to the State Apartments on the floor above. The staircase was moved for Queen Victoria in 1866 and the lobby fell into general disuse until its transformation into an exhibition space by the Royal Library in the 1960s.

The Castle Today

Windsor Castle's idyllic setting within the 5,700-acre Great Park and its proximity to London (just 20 miles/32 km) makes it an ideal weekend residence for The Queen. Here the Sovereign can spend some time off-duty, away from the rigours of court life, with family and friends enjoying quiet country pursuits in an informal atmosphere away from the public gaze.

The castle has been loved by The Queen since childhood. As a young princess the Sovereign was evacuated here to safety with her sister Princess Margaret when the bombs began to fall on London in 1940, and the princesses lived at Windsor throughout the Second World War.

Nowadays the Royal Family come to Windsor to enjoy outdoor activities, such as riding, carriage-driving, polo and shooting in the Great Park. Prince Charles often plays polo at Smith's Lawn during the season. Ascot week in June is greatly enjoyed, as well as the Royal Windsor Horse Show and the traditional Garter procession and service. All these events are highly popular with the public too, attracting huge crowds. The Royal Family usually spend part of the Christmas holiday at Windsor, when a party is held for the castle staff. At Windsor The Queen can offer hospitality to her ministers as well as representatives of foreign and Commonwealth countries. The castle is also a setting for great ceremonial occasions such as state visits or the gatherings of the Knights of the Garter.

TOP LEFT: *The Queen and competitors enjoying the Royal Windsor Horse Show.*

CENTRE LEFT: *The Queen and the Duke of Edinburgh arrive at Royal Ascot by carriage.*

BELOW LEFT: *Windsor en fête for a State Visit.*

ABOVE: *The South Front of Windsor Castle and the famous Long Walk. The Home Park provides a welcome retreat for The Queen and her family.*

RIGHT: *The Changing of the Guard on Castle Hill, beneath the Round Tower and the Royal Standard.*

PLAN OF THE CASTLE

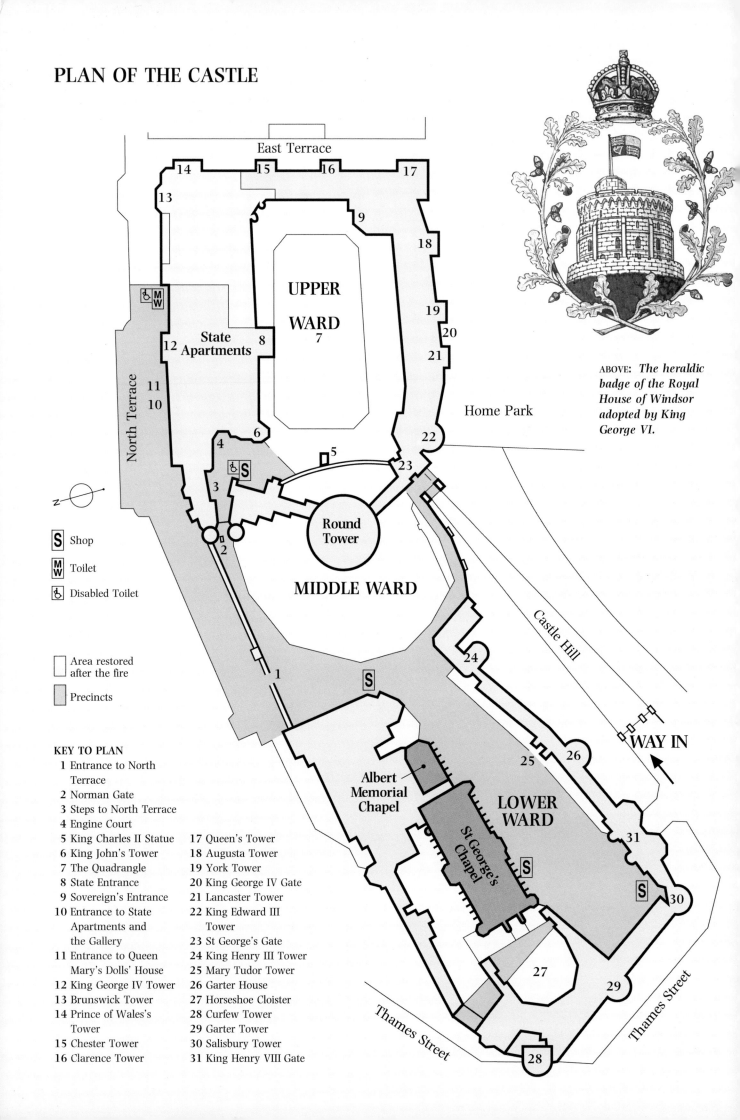

East Terrace

14 15 16 17

13

UPPER

WARD

7

9

18

19

20

21

State
Apartments
12 8

North Terrace

11
10

6

4

3

2

Round
Tower

MIDDLE WARD

22

Home Park

23

Castle Hill

24

WAY IN

25 26

31

30

Albert
Memorial
Chapel

St George's
Chapel

LOWER
WARD

27

29

28

Thames Street

Thames Street

ABOVE: *The heraldic
badge of the Royal
House of Windsor
adopted by King
George VI.*

S Shop

M
W Toilet

♿ Disabled Toilet

☐ Area restored
after the fire

Precincts

1

5

KEY TO PLAN

1 Entrance to North
 Terrace
2 Norman Gate
3 Steps to North Terrace
4 Engine Court
5 King Charles II Statue
6 King John's Tower
7 The Quadrangle
8 State Entrance
9 Sovereign's Entrance
10 Entrance to State
 Apartments and
 the Gallery
11 Entrance to Queen
 Mary's Dolls' House
12 King George IV Tower
13 Brunswick Tower
14 Prince of Wales's
 Tower
15 Chester Tower
16 Clarence Tower

17 Queen's Tower
18 Augusta Tower
19 York Tower
20 King George IV Gate
21 Lancaster Tower
22 King Edward III
 Tower
23 St George's Gate
24 King Henry III Tower
25 Mary Tudor Tower
26 Garter House
27 Horseshoe Cloister
28 Curfew Tower
29 Garter Tower
30 Salisbury Tower
31 King Henry VIII Gate